DID PRESIDENT HERBERT HOOVER

REALLY CAUSE THE GREAT DEPRESSION?

BIOGRAPHY OF PRESIDENTS

Children's Biography Books

Speedy Publishing LLC
40 E. Main St. #1156
Newark, DE 19711
www.speedypublishing.com

In this book, we're going to talk about the life of Herbert Hoover and whether he caused the Great Depression. So, let's get right to it!

Statue of Herbert Hoover in Minneapolis, Minnesota.

WHO WAS HERBERT HOOVER?

For one term, from 1929 through 1933, Herbert Hoover was the U.S. President. His presidency was marked by the 1929 crash of the stock market. This event triggered the Great Depression, which was a very difficult time for the people of the United States.

Herbert Hoover

Father, Jesse Clark Hoover
(1846–1880)

Mother, Hulda Minthorn Hoover
(1849–1883)

EARLY LIFE

Herbert Hoover was born in the Midwest state of Iowa. His father was a blacksmith. He came from a family of conservative Quakers. When he was very young, his parents both died and Herbert was sent to Oregon to live with his uncle when he was 10 years of age. He was a very intelligent, honest, and hard-working child.

Hoover earned his degree in geology at Stanford, a prestigious university in California. After he graduated, he got a job working for different mining companies around the world. He worked for a time in both China and Australia.

He was living in England when the First World War broke out. Americans who were still in Europe at the time were in danger, so Hoover personally helped over 120,000 United States citizens leave Europe and get home safely.

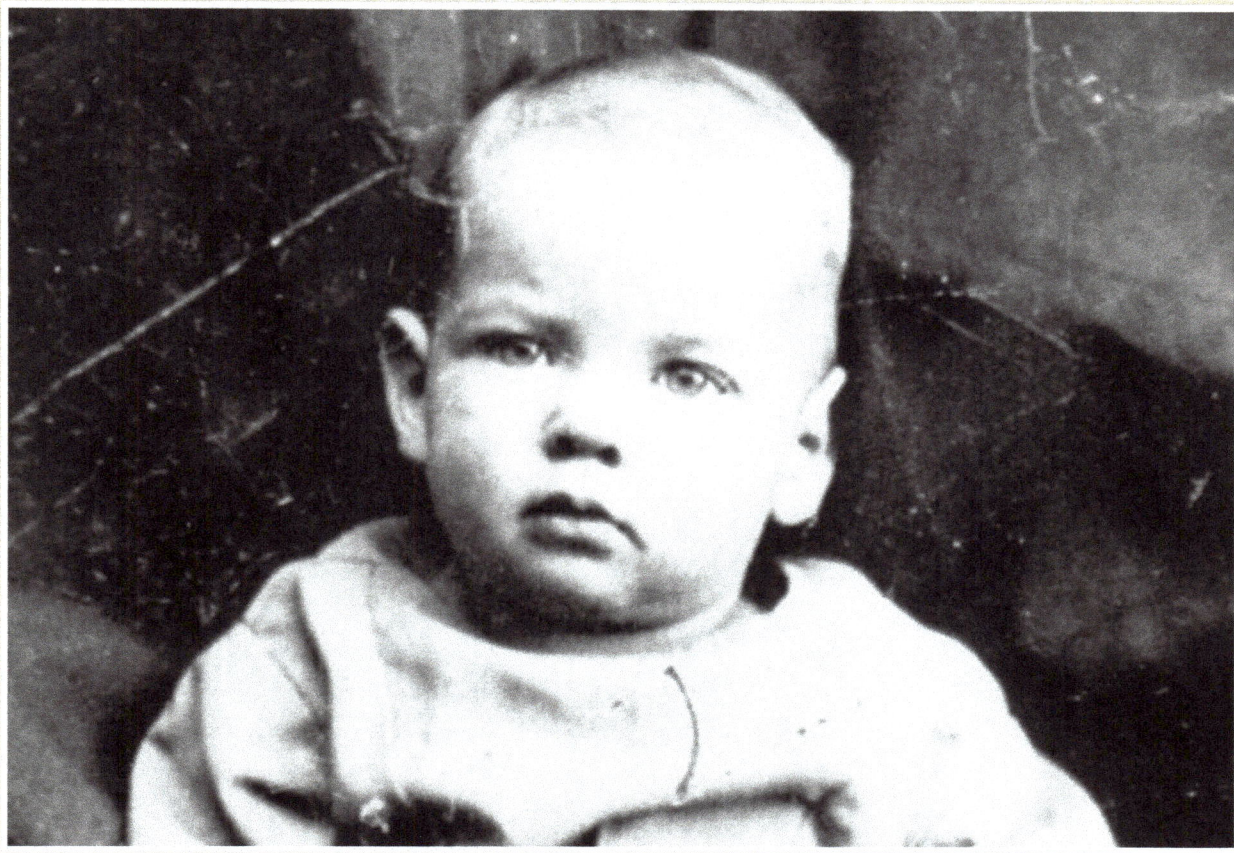

Herbert Hoover at age one.

WANTED
IMMEDIATELY
2,000,000
SEE DAILY PAPERS FOR COLLECTION CENTRES
GARMENTS
For destitute Men, Women and Children in
OCCUPIED NORTHERN FRANCE AND BELGIUM
Old or new clothing, dresses, underwear, shoes—wearing apparel of every kind.
CLOTHES COLLECTION WEEK
MARCH 25-30
Leave your bundle at nearest Red Cross Collection Center or any hand or steam Laundry
Under the auspices of the AMERICAN RED CROSS
Telephone Headquarters Greeley 5650

As the war progressed, he took a position helping to feed European refugees. His organization found a way to feed over 10 million people every day. His performance was so stellar that the United States President noticed his skills.

Clothing drive poster for those afflicted by WWI in Europe.

A MEMBER OF THE CABINET

When Warren Harding became president, he appointed Hoover to an important position in the cabinet, Secretary of Commerce. Unfortunately, Harding's presidency was filled with scandals and even though Harding was not involved his reputation was damaged.

Warren G.Harding (1865-1923), 29th President of the United States. 1921-1923.

Other cabinet members were involved in the scandals, but Hoover was an honest man and he wasn't involved in any of the criminal activity.

When Harding died of a heart attack, Calvin Coolidge took over as president and his first order of business was to *"Clean House."* Hoover stayed on as Secretary of Commerce during Coolidge's presidency.

President Calvin Coolidge waves a hat presented to him by the Smoki People of Prescott, Arizona.

He was placed in charge of numerous important public works projects. One such project was an amazing feat of engineering. It was located on the Colorado River and was originally named the Boulder Dam, but was eventually called the Hoover Dam in honor of Hoover.

Hoover Dam in Winter

HOOVER DAM

NAMED IN HONOR OF
HERBERT CLARK HOOVER
31st PRESIDENT OF THE UNITED STATES

U.S. DEPARTMENT OF THE INTERIOR

MARCH 3, 1849

Hoover was concerned about the *"out-of-control"* nature of the rising stock market and tried to warn Coolidge that more conservative economic policies were needed, but nothing was done and the stock market continued to rise.

Closeup of Hoover Dam sign at the Hoover Dam in Boulder City, Nevada.

Coming out of the Harding administration that had had so much scandal, Hoover had maintained his honest and hard-working reputation. The Republican Party sought him out to run for the next presidential election. Of the 48 states at that time, he won 40 of the states against the Democratic candidate Al Smith. Almost everyone wanted Hoover to be president.

Herbert Hoover as the new President, March 17, 1929,
by Oscar Cesare, original drawing.

Inauguration of President Hoover

HERBERT HOOVER AS PRESIDENT

Everything seemed to be going well for the United States and for Hoover, but several months into his presidency, events took an alarming turn. In the years prior to Hoover's election, the country had been experiencing an unprecedented economic boom. The economy had multiplied in value by more than a factor of six and the stock market had risen from 60 to 400.

oney was flowing like water and a lot of investors had quickly become millionaires. Even everyday people were placing mortgages on their properties and buying stocks with their life savings. The decade of peace and abundance before Hoover's election called *"The Roaring Twenties"* had lulled people into thinking that the stock market would always go up and that their money was safe.

A garden party during the 1920s.

The economy began to slow down a little, but the stock market was still on the upswing. People were buying stocks on margin, which simply means that they were borrowing money to buy the stocks to gain leverage and obtain more profits. Few people

understood that if their stocks lost value, they could lose all the money they invested plus owe significant amounts to their brokers. Most investors didn't realize that the stocks were overvalued and that what was happening was a stock market bubble.

Hoover tried to convince the managers on Wall Street that they needed to be more cautious, but his advice wasn't heeded.

The Federal Reserve raised the interest rates several times in an effort to dampen the intense rise of the market and allow it to stabilize, but what happened instead is that stocks began to go down in value and people started to get nervous.

A man at the stock exchange holding a ticker tape from the ticker machine.

They had had an increasing bull market for more than ten years and they didn't even realize that a decreasing bear market could happen. Fear started to spread and fear means panic. On Thursday, October 24, 1929, later called Black Thursday, the

stock market started to crash. The next day the market seemed to stabilize, but on the following Black Monday and Black Tuesday all was lost as 16 million shares were traded. The economic boom and wild times of the 1920s were over.

Many people who had never invested in the stock market were wiped out too. Banks had taken their deposits and placed them in stocks so the savings that people had carefully placed in the banks were wiped out as well. The stock market crash triggered the beginning of the Great Depression. This difficult time in American history continued for over a decade.

Bank patrons storming a bank.

Many people who had lost both their jobs and savings couldn't cope with their troubles and committed suicide. At one point over 30% of the people in the United States were living in poverty. In the cities, people stood in soup lines just to get something to eat so they wouldn't starve.

March on Washington of 10,000 unemployed men from Pittsburgh. Their leader, Father James Cos was received by President Herbert Hoover, January 7, 1932.

A year later, in the Great Plains, the Dust Bowl began. Intense drought had turned the topsoil to dust and gigantic dust storms traveled over the plains. It must have seemed like the end of the world to many people.

Farmer walking in dust storm Cimarron County, Oklahoma.

It took many years for the country to recover from the Great Depression. In 1939, the start of World War II expanded jobs and added to the economic recovery, but it was 1955 before the stock market returned to the level it had been before the crash.

Image of Lancaster bombers from Battle of Britain in World War Two.

THE IMPACT OF THE GREAT DEPRESSION ON HOOVER'S PRESIDENCY

The American people quickly forgot that they had elected Hoover in a landslide. They began to blame him for all the economic problems they were experiencing and the suffering they were going through. Camps were set up for the homeless and these shantytowns were nicknamed *"Hoovervilles."*

Bonus veteran army camp.

Shack colony at West and Charleton Streets
New York City

As a Republican, Hoover believed that the federal government shouldn't interfere in a large-scale way to manipulate the situation. Despite this, he did take action to get the country back on track. He put some large federal construction projects on the agenda to create some jobs. He also passed a sizable tax cut. He called upon industrialists and wealthy business owners to request their assistance.

In June of 1930, an important delegation of both bishops and well-connected bankers met with him to impress upon him that the situation was very dire. He assured them that the policies he had put in place

would speed up the nation's recovery. He was incorrect. Bank failures, unemployment, and bankruptcies continued to increase at an alarming rate. The country was in chaos with no relief in sight.

Herbert Hoover at Nine-Point Propserity Conference, 1932

When it was time for the next election in 1932, the American people were looking for a *"savior"* to step in and take action to improve things quickly. Since Hoover had not found a way to do this, he was blamed both for the occurrence of the Great Depression and also for not finding a way to make it end.

He campaigned on his record and at one point made the statement that things could actually be worse than they already were.

The democratic candidate Franklin D. Roosevelt promised to put plans in place to ensure that the economy would recover. In his message to the voters, he told them that his changes would guarantee that the *"Forgotten Man"* was no longer forgotten. Roosevelt won by a landslide because he offered the American people hope for a better future.

Herbert Hoover with Franklin D. Roosevelt, March 4, 1933.

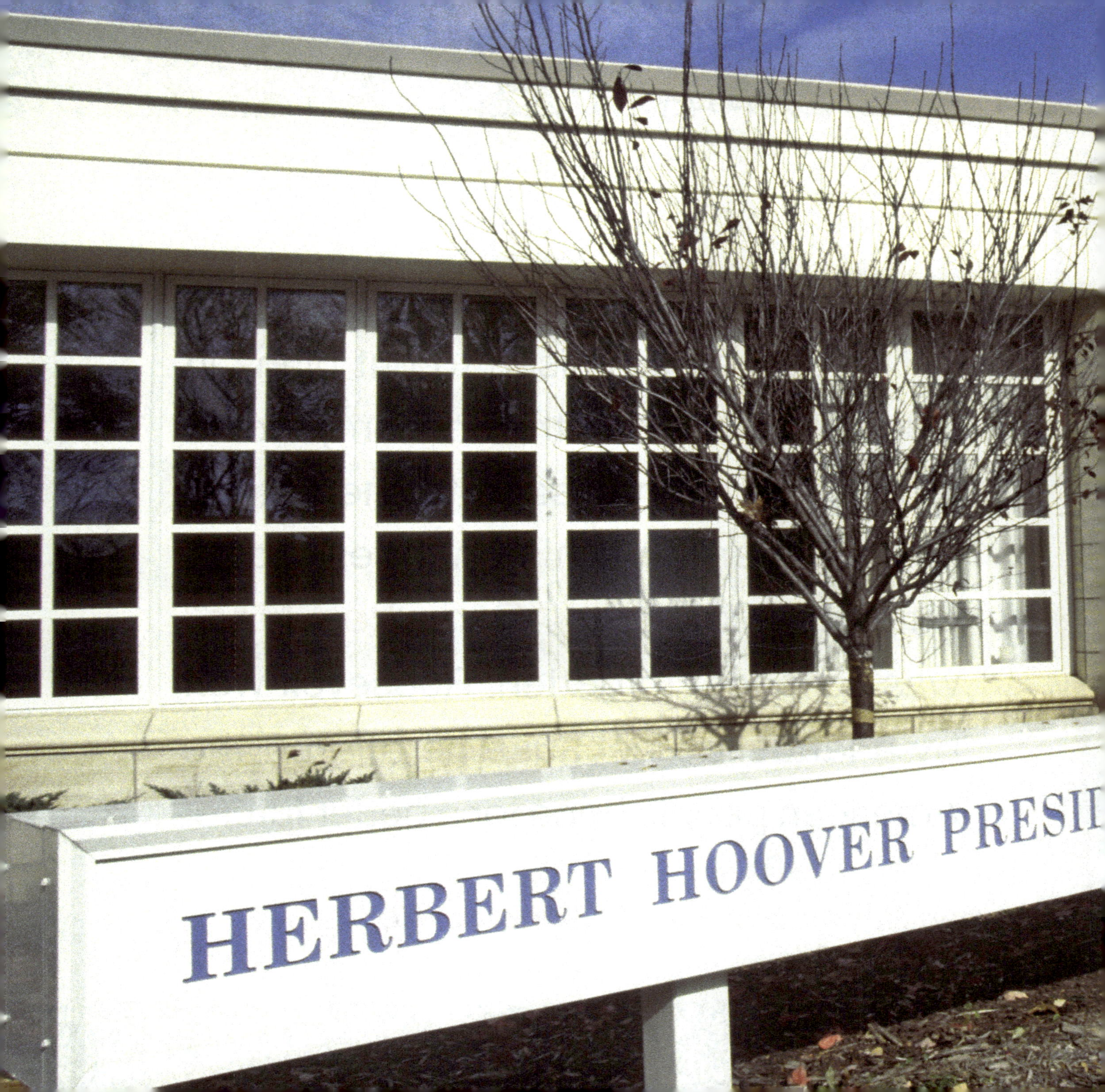
HERBERT HOOVER PRESI

NTIAL LIBRARY-MUSEUM

Herbert Hoover Presidential Library
Museum, West Branch, Iowa

AFTER THE PRESIDENCY

Despite all that he had been through, Hoover lived a full, useful life after he left the presidency. During the Second World War he helped with the needed food relief projects, just as he had during the First World War.

Herbert Hoover in his suite at the Waldorf Astoria Hotel.

He worked hand in hand with President Truman and later with President Eisenhower to find effective methods for cutting government spending. He passed away at the age of 90 after a life of public service to the country that he loved.

State Funeral for President Herbert Hoover, 1964.

Awesome! Now you know more about the life of President Herbert Hoover. You can find more Biography books from Baby Professor by searching the website of your favorite book retailer.

Painting of the birthplace of Herbert Hoover, West Branch, Iowa by artist Grant Wood.

Visit

BABY PROFESSOR
EDUCATION KIDS

www.BabyProfessorBooks.com

to download Free Baby Professor eBooks
and view our catalog of new and exciting
Children's Books

Milton Keynes UK
Ingram Content Group UK Ltd.
UKHW050919310824
447642UK00002B/39

9 798869 410870